This journal belongs to

....

*Y*ay, it's a new day.
It's going to be awesome!

*Y*ou found a parking spot in the front row. Yay! You saw a momma duck leading her little ducklings to a puddle. Yay! God answered your prayer for a friend. Yay! Your headache went away. Yay! You landed your dream job. Yay!

Life is a celebration when you count your blessings. This is the journal for all the events, accomplishments, simple blessings, and happy thoughts that make you think "Yay!" Keep lists, write stories, or pat yourself on the back.

You wrote in your journal—YAY!

*M*ay your heart hold sweet music
and may your eyes dance with joy.

*L*ife is a happy thing, a festival to be enjoyed.

Luci Swindoll

*S*mile so big that people wonder what you're up to.

*A*lways be on the lookout for the presence of wonder.

E. B. White

*E*ven a small drop of kindness can make a big splash in someone's day.

*Y*ou can't have everything. Where would you put it?

Steven Wright

A happy heart is like good medicine.

The Bible

*H*old puppies, kittens, and babies anytime you get the chance.

H. Jackson Brown Jr.

9 found it is the small everyday deeds of ordinary folk that keep the darkness at bay, small acts of kindness and love.

J. R. R. Tolkien

$\mathcal{S}$ometimes a spark of joy in your heart
is all it takes to light your way.

*I*f you look the right way,
you can see that the whole world is a garden.

Frances Hodgson Burnett

*Y*ou're off to great places, today is your day.
Your mountain is waiting, so get on your way.

Dr. Seuss

*S*pread love everywhere you go.
Let no one ever come to you without leaving happier.

Mother Teresa

I know that there is nothing better for people
than to be happy and to do good while they live.

The Bible

*W*hat a wonderful thought it is that some of the best days
of our lives haven't even happened yet.

Anne Frank

Remember this moment. Cherish this story. Celebrate this life.

*P*ractice random acts of kindness and senseless acts of beauty.

Jack Canfield

*B*eing happy never goes out of style.

Lilly Pulitzer

*I*f you stumble, make it part of the dance.

*H*e has made everything beautiful in its time.
He has also set eternity in the human heart.

The Bible

*Y*ou are amazing.
Remember that.

A single dream is more powerful than a thousand realities.

J. R. R. Tolkien

*I*t's kind of fun to do the impossible.

Walt Disney

*D*on't ever let anyone dull your sparkle!

*T*here are far, far better things ahead than any we leave behind.

C. S. Lewis

*H*e who began a good work in you will carry it on to completion.

The Bible

*I*f you have good thoughts they will shine out of your face
like sunbeams and you will always look lovely.

Roald Dahl

*T*here are so many beautiful reasons to be happy.

*R*emember how far you've come, not just how far
you have to go. You are not where you want to be,
but neither are you where you used to be.

Rick Warren

$\mathcal{S}$o far you've survived 100% of your worst days. You're doing great.

You are braver than you believe, stronger than you seem, smarter than you think, and loved more than you'll ever know.

A. A. Milne

*F*aith tells me that no matter what lies ahead, God is already there.

*B*elieve in yourself! Have faith in your abilities!
Without a humble but reasonable confidence
in your own powers you cannot be successful or happy.

Norman Vincent Peale

*S*he is clothed with strength and dignity
and she laughs without fear of the future.

The Bible

*T*he best and most beautiful things in the world cannot be seen
or even touched—they must be felt with the heart.

Helen Keller

_P_erhaps this is the moment for which you have been created.

*T*rust yourself. Create the kind of self that you will be happy
to live with all your life. Make the most of yourself by fanning the tiny,
inner sparks of possibility into flames of achievement.

Golda Meir

*T*he grass is always greener where you water it.

*S*ince you get more joy out of giving joy to others, you should put a good deal of thought into the happiness that you are able to give.

Eleanor Roosevelt

Go out of your way to be the light that brightens someone's day.

*T*he Lord will fight for you; you need only to be still.

The Bible

I'd far rather be happy than right any day.

Douglas Adams

*T*he idea is to die young, as late as possible.

*I*t was only a sunny smile, and little it cost
in the giving, but like morning light it scattered the night
and made the day worth living.

F. Scott Fitzgerald

Go big or go home.

*O*ptimism is a happiness magnet. If you stay positive, good things and good people will be drawn to you.

Mary Lou Retton

*Y*ou have it in you to outshine the brightest of stars.

*M*y grace is all you need.

The Bible

*I*f you are too busy to laugh, you are too busy.

$\mathcal{E}$ach day holds a surprise.

Henri Nouwen

*B*e a pineapple.
Stand tall, wear a crown, and be sweet on the inside.

*I*t is no bad thing to celebrate a simple life.

J. R. R. Tolkien

*M*ake today so awesome, yesterday gets jealous.

*T*he things you are passionate about are not random,
they are your calling.

Christine Kane

*Rejoice in everything you have put your hand to,
because the Lord your God has blessed you.*

The Bible

*T*oday was good. Today was fun.
Tomorrow is another one.

Dr. Seuss

*B*e the best part of someone's day.

_A_s soon as I saw you, I knew a grand adventure was about to happen.

A. A. Milne

A party without cake is just a meeting.

*H*appiness is letting go of what you think your life is supposed
to look like and celebrating it for everything that it is.

Mandy Hale

*N*ever miss a chance to laugh or make someone else happy.

I will be glad and rejoice in you;
I will sing the praises of your name, O Most High.

The Bible

*Y*ou only regret the things you didn't do.

*T*he best things in life are free, like sunshine, smiles,
and scoring that perfect parking spot at the grocery store.

*E*xpect nothing. Appreciate everything.

*T*hink of all the beauty still left around you and be happy.

Anne Frank

Life doesn't have to be perfect to be wonderful.

*D*ream big...don't let anybody or anything break your wishbone. Stay strong, full of faith, and courageous....And along the way, don't forget to laugh and enjoy the journey.

Charles R. Swindoll

*D*o not forget to show hospitality to strangers, for by so doing some people have shown hospitality to angels without knowing it.

The Bible

A single act of kindness throws out roots in all directions, and the roots spring up and make new trees. The greatest work that kindness does to others is that it makes them kind themselves.

Amelia Earhart

*B*e an instrument of God today—
let his song of love play through you.

If things are tough, remember that every flower that ever bloomed
had to go through a whole lot of dirt to get there.

Barbara Johnson

_S_ometimes a smile sneaks gently onto your face but other times
it bursts onto the scene like a marching band escaping from a clown car.

*L*et us think about each other and help each other
to show love and do good deeds.

The Bible

*Y*ou are never too old to set another goal
or to dream a new dream.

C. S. Lewis

*T*oss some confetti in the air and celebrate!

*A*bove all, watch with glittering eyes the whole world around you because the greatest secrets are always hidden in the most unlikely places. Those who don't believe in magic will never find it.

Roald Dahl

*Y*ou did well.... Come and share my joy with me.

The Bible

*I*f you can't make it better, you can laugh at it.

Erma Bombeck

*T*oday has the makings of the: Best. Day. Ever.

*Y*ou were made for strobe lights.

Angela Thomas

$\mathcal{S}$ilver linings are yours for the taking.

*T*he whole world is a love letter from God.

Peter Kreeft

*C*hocolate is made from beans. Beans are vegetables.
The recommended daily allowance
is five vegetables per day. Eat your veggies.

*T*he joy that you give to others is the joy that comes back to you.

John Greenleaf Whittier

*T*his is the day the Lord has made. We will rejoice and be glad in it.

The Bible

Ellie Claire® Gift & Paper Expressions
Franklin, TN 37067
EllieClaire.com
Ellie Claire is a registered trademark of Worthy Media, Inc.

YAY! Journal
© 2016 by Ellie Claire
Published by Ellie Claire, an imprint of Worthy Publishing Group, a division of Worthy Media, Inc.

ISBN 978-1-63326-153-2

Scripture in this journal is taken from: The Holy Bible, New International Version®, NIV®. Copyright © 1973, 1978, 1984, 2011 by Biblica, Inc.® All rights reserved worldwide. The Holy Bible, New Living Translation copyright © 1996, 2004, 2007 by Tyndale House Foundation. Used by permission of Tyndale House Publishers Inc., Carol Stream, Illinois 60188. All rights reserved. The New Century Version®. Copyright © 2005 by Thomas Nelson. Used by permission. All rights reserved.

Stock or custom editions of Ellie Claire titles may be purchased in bulk for educational, business, ministry, fundraising, or sales promotional use. For information, please e-mail info@EllieClaire.com.

Compiled and written by the YAY! Team: Bart, Marilyn, Melinda, m'lis, and Pamela
Art by Shutterstock | shutterstock.com

Printed in China.
3 4 5 6 7 8 9 10 11 RRD 23 22 21 20 19 18